A CHRISTMAS GIFT COLORING BOOK

GRAYSCALE ADULT COLORING BOOK OF OLD FASHIONED HOLIDAY SCENES

OLDE GLORIE STUDIOS

Merry Christmas

To:

From:

B·STUART

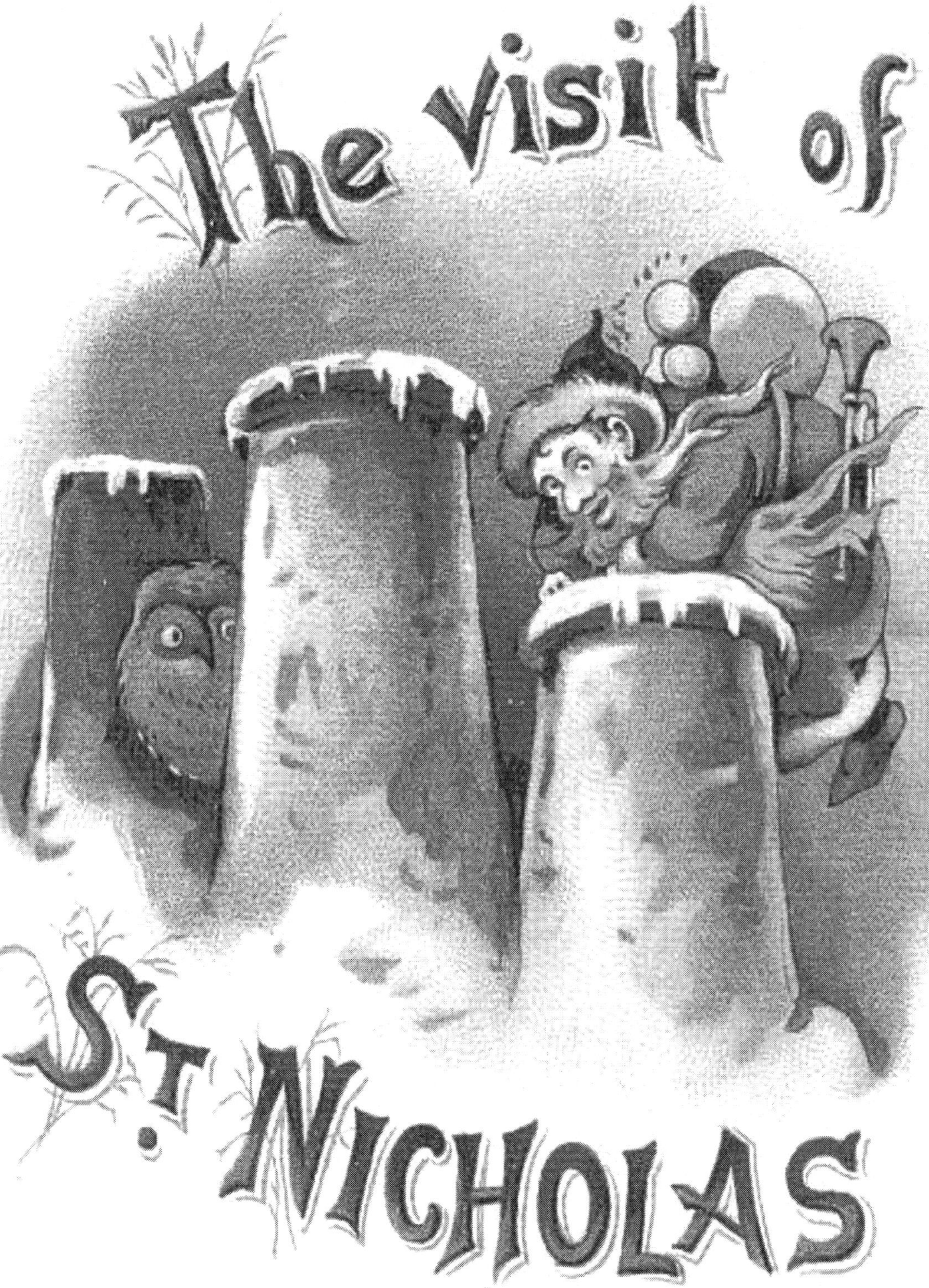
The visit of
St. Nicholas

Unto you is born this day in the city of David a Saviour, which is Christ the Lord.

A Winter
Morning

Christmas Greetings

A Merry Christmas.

December
25

A JOYFUL CHRISTMAS
TO YOU

A Merry Christmas

Christmas Greetings

May your Christmas Joys each year increase

The feet of the Christ-child
fall gentle and white.

Merry
Christmas!

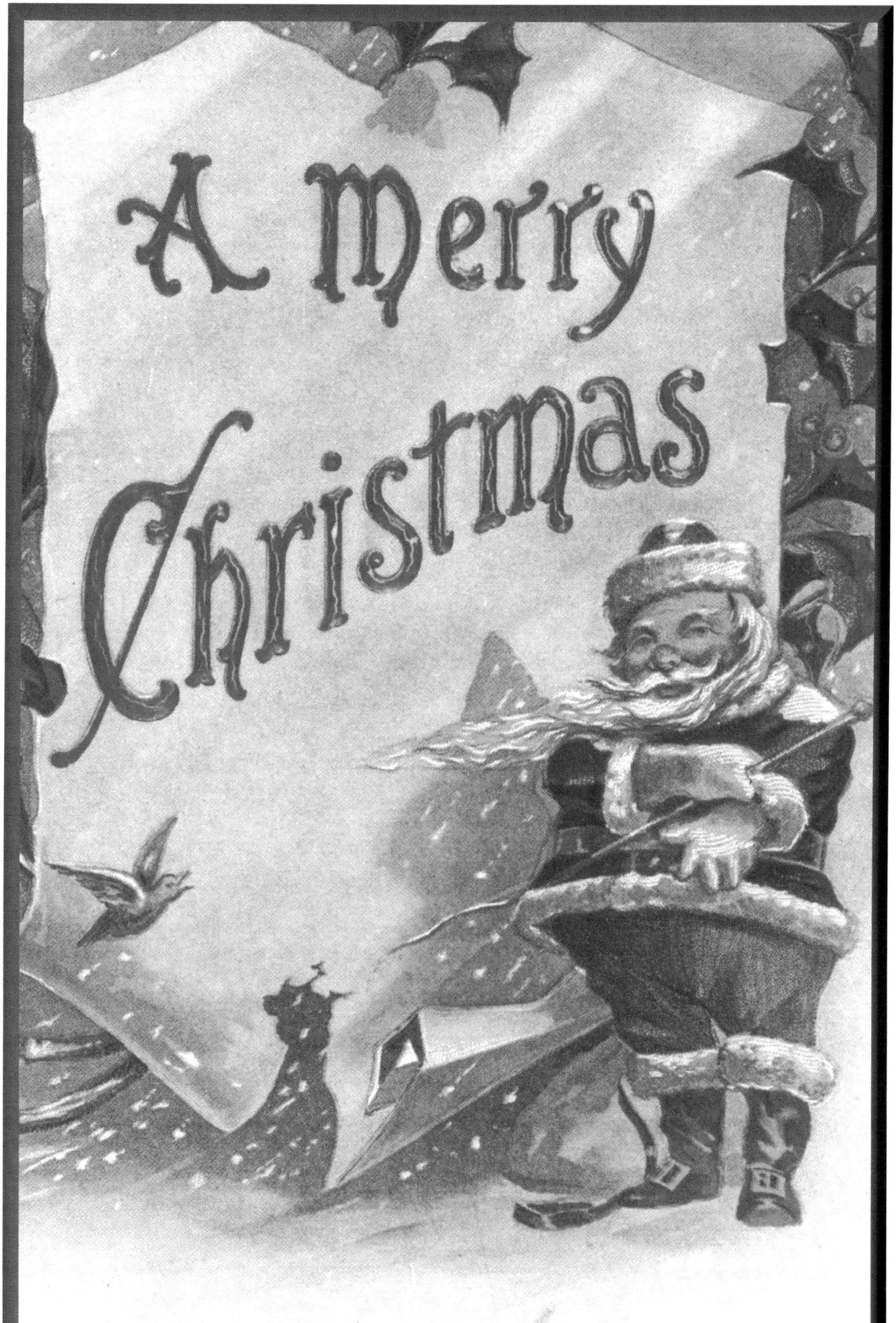
A Merry Christmas

No wish can hold a candle
In all the world so wide
Unto the one I send to you
This Merry Christmas-tide

A HAPPY CHRISTMAS

Made in the USA
San Bernardino, CA
07 October 2016